CAHAL B. DALY

Theologians and the Magisterium

Veritas Publications Dublin 1977

First published in 1977
in The Irish Theological Quarterly
and republished with the Editor's permission by
Veritas Publications,
7-8 Lower Abbey Street,
Dublin 1.

Cover design by Steven Hope

Printed by John English & Co., Ltd.,
Wexford

Cahal B. Daly is bishop of
Ardagh and Clonmacnois;
author of *Violence in Ireland* and
numerous contributions to
various magazines.

ISBN 0 905092 41 4
Cat. No.: 3360

In September 1966, an International Theological Congress was convened in Rome to study the theology of the Second Vatican Council. On the occasion of the Congress, Pope Paul addressed a letter to the participants and also delivered to them a significant discourse in the course of a concluding Audience. In both of these texts, Pope Paul developed an analysis of the role of the theologian in the Church which is still as relevant as it was then.

In his letter, the Pope began by discussing the limits which divine revelation and the unity of the faith impose upon the freedom of theologians. He then went on:

> But once these limits are recognised – and they are required by the very dignity of the Word of God, which of its nature is one and is everlasting – there remains an immense field of research where, as the Vatican Council put it, 'it is recognised that all the faithful, clerical and lay, possess a lawful freedom of inquiry and of thought, and the freedom to express their minds humbly and courageously about those matters in which they enjoy competence' (*Gaudium et Spes*, 62). It is precisely this lawful freedom which is the basis of progress in theology.[1]

Freedom is indeed a condition of all genuine progress in theology. But it is not in itself necessarily a guarantee of theological progress. It would be idle to deny that the new freedom given to Catholic theologians in recent years has been sometimes abused. Things have been written and said which have been quite simply a disgrace to Catholic theology. It often seems that much of the

---

[1] *Documentation Catholique*, 16 October 1966, col. 1733.

best work in theology is still being done by men formed in the older tradition and now themselves no longer young. The best fruits of freedom have, in many respects, still to be reaped.

The freedom which the Council sought to restore to all the members of the Church, and in particular to theologians, is a freedom in faith, a freedom to serve the believing community in the unity of charity which marks the body of Christ. This freedom calls for a greater sense of responsibility than ever on the part of all members of the Church. As freedom increased, the sense of personal responsibility was required to grow in keeping with it. As control by Church authority over the thinking and practice of Catholics diminished, the taking over by members of the Church, each in their own place and sphere, of personal responsibility for the purity of Catholic teaching and the fidelity of religious observance ought to have increased. When, for example, Church authority ceased to enforce the old regulations about prior theological control of religious writing, concern for the Catholic orthodoxy of the writing should have been taken over by writers themselves and by their theological colleagues, by editors, publishers, competent book critics, etc.

This sense of shared responsibility has not been always evident. One could list examples in all countries and languages of books and articles wholly irreconcilable with Catholic orthodoxy, utterly subversive of Catholic faith, or indeed of any Christian faith, which have been published with Catholic imprints or in Catholic periodicals, with no attempt by publisher or editor to offer comment or guidance to the reader, or even to provide adequate biographical information on which a non-specialist reader could himself base an informed judgment. Indeed the new liberty, instead of engendering a new sense of responsibility, has, it would seem, sometimes been used with the old mentality still anachronistically persisting. Incongruously, it seems as though some publishers or editors still assume that it is solely the bishops' duty to safeguard orthodoxy, and that a book or article can be presumed orthodox unless and until the bishops condemn it: or at least that the onus is on the Holy See to detect and call attention to heterodox teaching. Analogously, in a wider sphere, some Catholics seem to act as though any current behaviour can be presumed morally right unless and until the bishops or the priests condemn it. Catholics were rightly criticised in the past for waiting for bishops or priests to tell them what was right or wrong. When Church authority has radically and deliberately and rightly altered its whole mode of exercise, it is paradoxical to find the older attitude still persisting.

This is surely very far from the notion of responsible freedom and of the co-responsibility of all Christians for the unity of faith of the entire believing community, which were taught by Vatican II. It is very far indeed from the notion of the liberty of the Christian man so carefully and firmly proclaimed by St Paul and so clearly distinguished by him from irresponsible freedom or anarchic license. In the new age of Catholicism ushered in by the Council under the sign of Christian liberty, it would be, in the long term, impossible to preserve the unity of the Church, the soundness of the faith and the integrity of morals unless all members of the Church were to begin to feel themselves co-responsible with the Pope and the bishops, and co-responsible for one another, in respect of the faith and the unity and the Christian moral witness of the Church. The Church is now resolutely and irrevocably committed to the way of Christian freedom. It is urgently necessary for all of us in the Church to accept personal responsibility for using that freedom to build up the Church in faith and love.

Abuses of Authority
I have spoken of abuses of freedom. These are grave and have done serious harm to the Church. By and large, it is they, and not abuses of authority, which dominate the scene in the life of the Church since the Vatican Council. But it was not always so. There have been periods of the Church's history in the past, and even in the recent past, when it was not the liberty of theologians

but the power of authority which was abused. Much harm was done to the Church by these excesses and the consequences of the wounds are with us to this day. It is sad to recall some of the events of the years from the early 1940s to the late 1950s in the history of Catholic theology. It is humiliating to remember that some of the greatest names in modern Catholic theology were at one time under suspicion, if not for a time reduced to silence. Yet these were some of the very men whose pioneering work dominated the dramatic renewal of the Church's theology and spirituality and life effected by the Second Vatican Council.

All was by no means black in those times. The work of theological, scriptural and biblical renewal went on. Pope Pius XII, both by example and by exhortation and patronage, gave powerful impetus to scriptural and theological progress. Pope John XXIII never failed to hail in him the great intellectual and pastoral precursor of Vatican II. None of those affected by the climate of official fear and suspicion wavered for a moment in faith or in loyalty to the Church. Many echoed words of Father de Lubac, that truly to love the Church is to be prepared to suffer from her. Indeed the paradox is that more progress in theology was made in that period than in other decades which were humanly speaking more propitious to progress. This however is what we should expect; for theological renewal, like every form of Christian life, must be marked by the mystery, which is also the scandal, of the Cross.

Nevertheless, this recent experience is certainly one element in the present malaise and confusion within the Church. It is understandable that some of the more aggressive of the younger theologians today should be militantly determined to vindicate the new-found freedom of theology. It is understandable that they should be vigilant lest similar abuses of authority should ever be allowed to recur. It is understandable that they should be hypersensitive regarding any act of the magisterium which seems to constitute any restriction of their freedom. It is also a fact that this experience of the past has made it more difficult for some to distinguish legitimate and necessary exercises of the contemporary magisterium from regrettable acts of it in the past. One result is that some will argue that, if theologians who were suspect twenty-five years ago are in the main stream of orthodoxy now, then theologians who today are suspect may be simply anticipating now the orthodoxy of twenty years from now.

The argument is plausible but wholly superficial. The very theologians who led the renewal movement of twenty-five years ago have been and are among the first to dissociate themselves from some of the pretended theologians of renewal who now invoke their example. The pioneers have not changed direction; but they see that many who claim to carry on their movement are in fact moving away in a different direction entirely, a direction which would not only abandon the heritage of centuries of Catholic tradition but would reverse the immense progress of the past thirty years. Further, we have only to compare the work of the great men of the 1930s and the 1940s with that of some who today claim to be the theologians of the future, in order to see on which side lies the balance of biblical and patristic scholarship, of science and learning and spirituality. Above all, one can easily detect in the great pioneers the humility, the serenity and the charity which always distinguish the saint from the mere professional, or simply mark off the great man from the small.

It is salutary for us all to contrast the shrillness with which some today speak of the sad events of the 1940s and the serenity with which the men who actually suffered from these events themselves speak of them. The actual sufferers of twenty-five years ago were enhanced in their persons and strengthened in their faith and their love of the Church – the correct word is sanctified – by their nobility in suffering. The men who today presume vicariously to avenge them are diminished in their persons and damaged in their thinking by their very bitterness. We can all of us benefit by remembering that Father de Lubac's *Splendour of the Church* was written in the midst of his personal trial; that the chapter entitled 'Mater Ecclesia', in which he treats of obedience, was published in advance, in an article in *Études*, in the very midst of the storm attending the crisis of the priest-worker movement in France. We can all of us profit by reading Father Congar's own conclusion in his 'Reflections and Souvenirs 1929-1973', to his description of the sad years:

> If I was able to survive spiritually, and even from the point of view of physical health, I was able to do so only by the full acceptance of the Cross and of reduction to nothingness . . . . I have often thought of the words of St Paul: 'Suffering brings patience and patience brings hope' (*Romans* 5:4). One would expect him to put it the other way round: it would seem that hope is the basis for patience. In one sense this is true. But the order St Paul follows conveys a still deeper truth. Those who do not know how to suffer do not know how to hope either. Men who are too much in a hurry; men who want to gain their ends immediately, cannot hope either . . . .
>
> The Cross is a condition of every holy work. God himself is at work in what is for us a cross. It is in this way only that we ourselves arrive at any authenticity and depth of existence. Nothing is fully serious until one is prepared to pay this price for it. 'There are areas of our poor heart which do not exist yet; and they will begin to exist only when suffering enters them' (Léon Bloy). Only he who has suffered for his convictions gives these convictions a certain strength, a certain quality of irresistibleness; at the same time, only he earns for himself a right to be respected and to be listened to. O Crux Benedicta.[2]

BALANCE BETWEEN AUTHORITY AND LIBERTY

As Father Roderick MacKenzie remarks, 'Abuses of liberty do not prove that liberty is a bad thing, any more than abuses of authority

---

[2] Yves Congar: *Une Passion: L'unité Reflexions et Souvenirs* 1929-1973. coll. Foi Vivante, Cerf, Paris 1974, pp. 80-84.

prove the same about authority.'[3] The sad events I have referred to should be enough to make us pause before talking nostalgically of 'the good old days' or before hoping for their return. Yet, whatever about the past, it is in the present that we are called to witness for Christ. It can scarcely be questioned that today the pendulum has swung decisively in the opposite direction. The balance of popular opinion and emotion today are heavily weighted against authority. This is true, of course, not only in the Church but also in secular society; but the implications for the Church, given the essential, divinely appointed hierarchical structure of the Church, are particularly momentous.

The new situation creates novel problems for those entrusted with responsibility for teaching and pastoral guidance and government in the Church. The fact is that, even when theologians do not formally claim to be a 'parallel magisterium' – and very few would in fact advance any such claim – they are *de facto* often treated and quoted as if they were. The media have an important role here. Authority in the Church is never nowadays given the last word; indeed rarely allowed even to have an unchallenged first word. Every pronouncement of Pope or bishops is always presented in parallel with the comment and glosses of theologians upon it. Indeed, because of the irresistible attraction which conflict and dissent have for those who work in media, the first theologians invited to comment on any statement of the magisterium will often be those who are known in advance to be likely to dissent and contest. A situation naturally grows in which the teaching of the Church's magisterium is regarded as depending for its validity on the consensus of theologians. Indeed, this or that theologian will occasionally claim for views rejected by the magisterium the support of an 'emerging consensus', thus setting a suppositious 'Church of the future' against the real Church of the present. In ways like this theologians come to be accepted in

---

[3] Article, 'Function of Scholars in forming the judgment of the Church', in *Theology of Renewal*, Palm Publishers, Dorval, Quebec 1968, vol. II, pp. 125-6.

some sectors of opinion as a sort of *de facto* 'alternative magisterium'.

This reversal of the balance between magisterium and theologians has far-reaching implications, not only for bishops, but also, I suggest, for theologians themselves. It is vital for the work of both and for the service of either to the Church that new forms of relationship and of working together be found between them. So far as we bishops are concerned, it has, I suggest, to be accepted that no episcopal statement will in fact appear unattended by theologians' commentary. It is, therefore, in the interests of the effectiveness of their teaching itself that, as far as possible, bishops consult with theologians in advance if issuing statements on matters in which theologians have competence.

This is by no means merely an attempt to pre-empt the support of theologians. It is desirable in order to ensure, in collaboration, the best possible theological substance and scriptural grounding and scientific accuracy for the statement. It is desirable also in order to ensure that theologians are given the opportunity of contributing their gifts of 'wisdom' and 'knowledge' (St Paul's terms are *sophia* and *gnosis*) to the wellbeing of the Church. It is in this way that theologians are enabled to practise co-responsibility, according to their competence, with the bishops for the faith of the Church.

Theologians need the Magisterium

This consultation is not only for the benefit of bishops. It is for the benefit of theologians as well. Theology can never be solely a professional pursuit, an academic discipline or a university career. Theology is reasoned discourse about God; but discourse is not about God unless it springs from faith in him and leads to love and worship and service of him. Neither faith nor love nor worship nor service of God are possible except in relation to the community of believers and worshippers which is the

Church. Theology is service of the Church, or else it should have some other name, like philosophy of religion, comparative religion, or whatever. Theology, therefore, without an ecclesial dimension, a liturgical and spiritual expression and a pastoral orientation is defective *as theology*. Professor Hans Kueng put this well in a little book published in 1965. He wrote:

> All the leading Catholic theologians today earnestly desire to be truly representative of the Church; they want to have the Church behind them in their theology; they want to do theology *for* the Church and *in* the Church. A theology, then, that is, first, *for* the Church: at once scientific in character and pastoral in orientation; and, second, a theology that is *in* the Church: at once critical in outlook and ecclesially committed.
>
> Today's theological renewal . . . does bear a wholly and entirely ecclesial stamp. Its desire is to be a theology *in* the Church. Its leading theologians do not take up a sceptical or resigned attitude on the periphery of the Church's life; their position is one of total conviction, right in the centre of the Church . . . . They want to do their theology not only *for* her, but also *in* her. They are well aware that the subject-matter on which they work is not something they have discovered but something they have received . . . . [God's Word] has come to them by the testimony, tradition, and proclamation of the great community of believers . . . .[4]

These desiderata once expressed by Hans Kueng are, as we shall see, quite similar to the directives offered by Pope Paul. They are most likely to be realised in the context of two-way collaboration between theologians and the hierarchy.

Despite the difficulties sometimes experienced by theologians in the past at the hands of authority, Catholic theologians have derived immense benefit and strength from the distinctive under-

[4] Hans Kueng, *The Theologian and the Church*, coll. Theological Meditations, Sheed and Ward, London 1965 (the German original was first published in 1964), pp. 4, 17-18.

standing of their place in the Church which characterises the Catholic tradition and even from the service sought from them in the Church's practice. Their place tended, in most places, to be in seminaries rather than in universities; and, although this had drawbacks, it kept theologians closer to the people of God and involved them in the pastoral and spiritual as well as the intellectual formation of priests. Both of these factors gave the work of theologians the pastoral and spiritual and liturgical dimensions which it could otherwise have lacked. Theologians were never likely to forget that there are other ways of knowing God than the intellectual way; other forms of expertise in relation to God than the expertise of the theologian, other languages about God than the language of theology. Entrusted with the formation of priests, theologians by definition enjoyed an honoured place in the Church, entailing confidence from the hierarchy, standing among priests, respect from the people.

It is indeed important to ensure that theology takes its due place in university studies. This will be for the good of theology; for theology is the most rigorous and demanding exercise which it is given to human reason to pursue, and it can only profit by association with men whose profession is the development of reason and the pursuit of truth. This will also be to the benefit of university studies; for however many the scientific disciplines cultivated in a university campus and however high the standards achieved in them, reason will not have been seen in its whole range and power until it has been seen wrestling with God and confronting all the languages and sciences of man with the science of God's Word.

But it will be vital to ensure that association with universities is not allowed to deprive theology of the other associations without which it cannot remain true to itself. Faith is not only a problem to be solved; it is also a gift from God, to be accepted in simplicity and joy. It is a life to be lived in love. It is 'a lamp lighting the way through the dark', a little night-light, but quite enough for us 'until the dawn comes' (2 *Peter* 1:19). It is a grace

and privilege to be received with humble and contented thankful-
ness. One of the temptations of modern Christians is to think
that it is 'in their much speaking' that God is to be found: that
is to say that the approach to God is mainly through words,
argument, and discussion. Their error could be analogous to
that of those whose self-assertive way of praying our Lord
rebuked. In an age of much verbalisation, indeed of verbal
inflation, we must learn again the power of non-verbalised
commitment, the commitment of a faith whose power and energy
come from love, simplicity, childlike acceptance, confidence and
joy. It is vital that theologians engage in dialogue with those to
whom faith is a problem, a disquiet, an emptiness. But it is
vital that theologians bring to the dialogue a quiet, humble,
simple certitude, a fullness that they have received from Christ
and from those who have seen Christ's glory. For this, it is
essential that theologians listen to and learn from those who have
not asked to 'see [Jesus Christ] yet love him; and still without
seeing him are filled with a joy so glorious that it cannot be
described, because they believe and are sure of the end to which
[their] faith looks forward' (1 *Peter* 1 : 8-9).

The times when theology had least credibility in the Catholic
Church tended to be the times when it was most academic, most
university-enclosed, most out of touch with the pastoral clergy
and their sacramental service of the Christian community, most
out of contact with religious, both active and contemplative, and
most removed from the believing and praying people. One
such period was the fourteenth and fifteenth centuries; and the
attitude of Thomas à Kempis to theology and theologians in his
Imitation of Christ shows how poor their standing then was.

There are, however, few parallels in Catholic history to the
scorn which Kierkegaard reserves for theologians as he would
have known them in the Protestant tradition, that is to say,
theologians occupying university chairs in the Germanic and
Nordic lands. With withering irony he asks in his *Journal*:

Why is it that we couldn't help bursting out laughing if some-

one were to read St Paul's list of gifts within the Church to
the effect that God gave a place to prophets and a place to
apostles and a place to leaders of the community . . . but
went on to add 'and a place to professors of theology'![5]
Involvement with the bishops in the pastoral applications of
theology will, therefore, help both to preserve to theology its
indispensable pastoral character and to ensure to theologians
their place both of service and of honour in the Church of Christ.

THE ROLE OF THE MAGISTERIUM

There are other and even profounder reasons why theologians
need the magisterium. Only the magisterium can, by Christ's
ordination, judge in final analysis of the faith of the community.
But unless theology is the explicitation, and connatural, authentic
development, but never the subversion, of the faith of the community, then it is only human speculation and has no more
right than any other human science to be listened to by the
Church.

It is false to label the hierarchical magisterium 'a pastoral
magisterium' and to contrast it with a 'doctrinal magisterium'
reserved to the theologians. By Christ's institution, the pastoral
magisterium of bishops is also doctrinal. The first duty of pastors
in the Church is to feed the faith of their people with sound
doctrine. 'Pastoring' is, before and above all else, teaching. The
duty to teach is, in the New Testament, the primary and distinctive mandate of the apostles and of their successors. By
Christ's ordinance, they, and not directly the theologians, enjoy
the assurance of the guidance and assistance of the Holy Spirit for
this teaching mandate. Theologians and others in the Church
enjoy this assurance only within a Church which Christ endowed
with a hierarchical structure and a Spirit-guided papal and
episcopal magisterium. To 'proclaim the message and, welcome

----

[5] Cited in G. Chantraine, *Vraie et fausse liberté du theologien*, Desclée de
Brouwer, Paris 1969, p. 72.

or unwelcome, insist on it . . . with patience and with the intention of teaching' (2 *Timothy* 4:2), is the hierarchy's task and not their choice; it is their burden and not their boast. This they cannot surrender to the theologians or to anyone else, because they received it from God and not from men, and they 'must obey God rather than men' (*Acts* 4:19).

The hierarchical magisterium exists in Christ's Church, not to give any special group access to a 'power base', but to ensure for the Church the only base of power she has ever had or needed, the power of Christ's word. The teaching function of the Pope and the bishops is a service to the Church, the greatest and most indispensable service that can be given to her, the service of keeping her members, both hierarchy and people, submissive to the Word of God. Aquinas expressed as follows the role of the Papal Primacy:

> Christ, the Son of God, consecrates his Church by his Holy Spirit and places on her the mark of his spiritual seal. In a corresponding way, the role of the Vicar of Christ and the significance of his primacy and his office are that, as a faithful servant, he should keep the whole Church submissive to Christ.[6]

Most of the pronouncements of the magisterium are simply recalls of the existing binding statements of the Church's faith, what Kueng has called 'the decisive statements of faith'. To such a pronouncement it is no retort to say that it fails to mark progress in theology. Theology is not the measure of faith but is itself measured by faith. There can be no progress in theology except *within* 'the obedience of faith' and never beyond it.

When the magisterium points out that a theological hypothesis contradicts a binding statement of the Church's faith, again it is no retort that this is restricting theological freedom. When the Church has staked her existence as a believing community on a certain formula, then the truth contained in that formula is known for all time to carry the guarantee of Christ's indefectible

---

[6] *Contra errores Graecorum*, 16.

promise of truth. Cultural change, scientific progress, etc., may bring it about that that same truth can be more accurately expressed to a later generation in other terms. The Church, guided by the Holy Spirit, may also come to enter further into the depths of mystery contained in that truth. Any new formulation, any development of doctrine, must always preserve undamaged the truth-content of the original binding statement. There can be no question of a 'development' of doctrine which contradicts the truth-content of an earlier dogmatic formulation of the Church. The reason is that that formulation was built on the rock of Christ's truth-promise to his Church. There can be no theological progress, no authentic theological freedom, against Christ's truth. Rahner put this memorably when, speaking of transubstantiation, he said:

> Since the dogma of transubstantiation, even in its explicit formulation, has stood for centuries in the faith of the Church, the Church would have had to deny its own being, as it understood itself to be, if it gave up this doctrine.[7]

The guidance which, in the context of faith, the theologian receives from the magisterium creates in fact a context of freedom within which he is sure, not just of achieving intellectual satisfaction through the pursuit of his science, but of penetrating the unfathomable mysteries of God. This guidance also gives others in the Church the assurance that, in listening to or reading a theologian they are indeed being put in touch with God. This is the very meaning of the theologian's role in the Church, and the explanation of why it is precisely through the Church that he has his role and his standing and his following. The people desire and have the right to be assured that when they follow the opinion of a theologian they are following Christ and listening to his words of eternal life. If a theologian cut himself off from

---

[7] Art. 'Christ in the Sacrament of the Lord's Supper', in *Theological Investigations*, vol. IV, *More Recent Writings*, Darton, Longman and Todd, London 1966, p. 297.

this contact with the magisterium he would deprive himself of credibility.

What I have been saying is quite close to views once expressed by Hans Kueng, in the little book I have previously cited. He said:

> Theologians have no desire to be some species of free-floating thinkers, historians, or dealers in speculative ideas, belonging nowhere and hence bound to nobody. What point would there be in their existence as theologians, without the Church? They want to do their theology not only *for* her but also *in* her. . . . Right from her beginning, and on through the centuries, the Church continues to be, in her teaching, the bearer of this witness of faith filled with the Spirit.
>
> Hence any theology which desires to appeal, as Christian theology, to that witness of faith, has always got to grow out of the Church as the community of believers, so as to be of service to her and hence to the world. Without the community of believers it loses its context and its goal . . . . It is through the Church, through her *confessions of faith* and *definitions*, made as delimitations against heresy in various historical situations, that the individual theologian is helped in finding the difficult road of faith between the different varieties of false belief, superstition and unbelief. History shows that a theologian cannot with impunity despise the fences and the danger signs which the Church of former ages, in her battle to defend the one true faith, has set up to distinguish good from bad interpretations of the message, often in times of extreme urgency and danger.[8]

A Catholic theologian who is thinking and working critically is not restricted in his freedom, but he is protected against arbitrariness by his dependence on the faith of the community of the Church. It is precisely this fact that he stands in the midst of the believing community of the Church that preserves him in *true* freedom. He is safeguarded against making the

[8] Hans Kueng, *The Theologian and the Church*, pp. 18-19.

results of his research into absolutes. He is made aware of his own inescapable character and limitations, which is very much to the benefit of his theology. This makes him free for the ever-surpassing truth of God's Word. . . . He will never on principle confront the Church's belief with distrust, but, whatever critical scrutiny and argument he may make, he will always reverently and confidently take as his starting-point that God's Word has never been without witness in his Church nor ever will be; that it is through her, the Church as a community, that the Lord's promises were given.[9]

The Magisterium needs Theologians

But the hierarchical magisterium in turn needs the help of theologians. The conditions of a bishop's life today leave little time for study; and outside the context of a life of scholarship it is impossible nowadays to be adequately informed about the immense new 'explosion of knowledge' which characterises theology and all the sacred sciences, like all the human sciences, today. Without the help of scholars, bishops would find it difficult to keep abreast of the new knowledge and to mobilise it for the service of the Gospel. It is true that the teaching role of bishops is distinct and inalienable: it cannot as such be shared with theologians. Bishops must reserve the right – precisely because they have the solemn duty – to teach and to speak independently of theologians, and even to reject theologians' advice when convinced in conscience that this is necessary. Authentic statements of the episcopal magisterium must be and be seen to be exercises of the divinely appointed teaching authority in the Church, and not merely the opinions of theologians, or even reflections of the 'consensus of theologians'. Nevertheless, the relationship of bishops and theologians must not be allowed to be one of mutual distance, distrust or suspicion, but one of fraternal collaboration in mutually complementary service of the Church of Christ, the Mother of us all, in whom we all believe and whom we all love.

[9] Hans Kueng, *The Theologian and the Church*, pp. 30-31.

One could not express this relationship better than Pope Paul has done in the text to which I referred at the outset. He said:

Theology has a twofold relationship with the magisterium of the Church and with the Christian community as a whole. Theology is, in a certain sense, a mediator between the faith of the Church and the magisterium. Theology gleans the living faith of the Christian community, its truths, its emphases, its problems, the aspirations which the Holy Spirit arouses in the people of God ('what the Spirit says to the Churches' [*Apoc*, 2:7]). Theology has carefully to examine this living faith and its orientations with the criteria of a sound theological method, measuring it by the touchstone of the Word of God and the whole tradition of the Church. . . . In this way, theology can help the magisterium to be at all times the light and the guide of the Church . . .

Theology has still another function in relation to the magisterium: It is a mediator of the magisterium's teaching for the formation of the faith and the moral life of the Christian people . . .

Without theology, the magisterium would lack the instruments which are essential for the conducting of the great symphony in which the entire Church community express their thinking and their living in Jesus Christ . . .

Theologians are and should be very happy to know that they are at the service of the Christian community and of the magisterium. Their task is an integral part of the great task of the Church – the salvation of souls. Their greatness does not consist in advancing novel ideas and doctrines, but rather in the ceaseless preoccupation to speak 'the words of eternal life', in such a fashion that they enter deeply into souls and lead them to the point of personal commitment to faith in Jesus Christ, our only Saviour.[10]

Pope Paul concluded his allocution by saying:

The magisterium draws immense benefit from the fervent

---

[10] *Documentation Catholique*, 16 October 1966, col. 1738-1739.

activity of theologians and from cordial collaboration with them. . . . Without the help of theology, the magisterium could undoubtedly preserve and proclaim the faith; but it would have great difficulty in acquiring that full and deep knowledge which it needs in order fully to accomplish its task.[11]

In his letter to the same Theological Congress, the Pope had called for a theology which would be both pastoral and scientific:

The Council exhorts theologians to develop a theology which will be at once pastoral and scientific; a theology which will be closely in contact with the sources, both patristic, liturgical and particularly biblical; a theology which will always have profound respect for the magisterium of the Church and in particular the magisterium of the Vicar of Christ; a theology which will be relevant to human existence as historically lived and as actually experienced; a theology which will be openly ecumenical, but at the same time openly and sincerely Catholic.[12]

Hans Kueng's words in 1965 were very close to those of Pope Paul, when he called for:

a theology that is, first, *for* the Church: at once scientific in character and pastoral in orientation; and, second, a theology that is *in* the Church: at once critical in outlook and ecclesially committed.

Hans Kueng at that time made a moving plea for humility on the part of theologians:

It follows from this that the individual theologian does not try to force the results of his studies on the community of the Church. He does not want it to be his doctrine that dominates in the Church anymore than anyone else's. He will on the contrary try to be of service in the Church by laying the results of his work before the Church so that she can tell whether or not she can recognise in them her own belief, the belief of

[11] *Ibid.*, col. 1738.
[12] *Documentation Catholique*, col. 1732.

the whole community. Hence the theologian will seek discussion. He will be ready to be corrected and refuted. He will not think himself alone in the truth or equate his words with the word of God . . . Hence the theologian who is thinking and working critically will always and everywhere have plenty of grounds for humility.[13]

Pope Paul asked theologians to be

conscious of the limitations of their own talents and careful always to respect the opinions of others, and particularly of those whom the Church recognises as the most reliable witnesses and interpreters of her doctrine.[14] [He is referring here, following the Vatican Council's Declaration on Christian Education, to 'the Doctors of the Church, and particularly St Thomas Aquinas'.][15]

It is, in particular, important that theologians, instead of dividing into separate and non-communicating compartments marked 'conservative' and 'progressive,' should dialogue with one another across these much-abused classifications. Provided that there is genuine scholarship and genuine love of the Church on both sides, each of these orientations has much to learn from the other. For one thing, much of the sheer silliness of the secularising theologians could never have survived into print if it had first been discussed with responsible theologians trained in the classical tradition. Furthermore, the classically trained and more conservative-minded have nothing to lose and much to gain, as well as much to contribute, in dialogue with theologians more familiar with newer scholarship and more open to newer insights. All the great theologians of the classical tradition believed theology to be a progressive science and the greatest of them were in their day themselves criticised as innovators. It is significant that Hans Kueng gives St Thomas Aquinas as his model for the progressive theologian.[16]

---

[13] *The Theologian and the Church*, p. 4.
[14] *Op. cit.*, p. 31.
[15] *Documentation Catholique*, col. 1733.
[16] *Op. cit.*, p. 52.

In any case, it is time for theologians to drop the schoolboy habit of calling names at one another. The problems of the Church today are too serious and her need for the help of all her theologians too urgent for this. Attaching labels to individuals or to groups of theologians is too like the spirit of faction which Pope Paul deplored in the Church in Corinth. Here various factions had their slogans and leaders: ' "I am for Paul"; "I am for Apollos"; "I am for Cephas" '. . . . Paul asks: 'What is the meaning of all these slogans? Has Christ been parcelled out?' He appeals for an end to such cliques and lobbies, and we can all take his words to heart:

> I do appeal to you brothers, for the sake of our Lord Jesus Christ, to make up the differences between you and instead of disagreeing among yourselves to be united again in your beliefs and practice (1 *Corinthians* 1:10).

Elsewhere, speaking to the Galatians, he warns still more gravely – and the words once more are strikingly relevant to our age of greater liberty for theologians and for all members of the Church:

> My brothers, you were called, as you know, to liberty; but be careful, or this liberty will provide an opening for self-indulgence. . . . If you go on snapping at each other and tearing each other to pieces, you had better watch or you will destroy the whole community (*Galatians* 5:13, 15).

DEFENCE OF THEOLOGIANS BY THE MAGISTERIUM

Since the contribution of theologians is so vital to the Church nowadays, it is an important pastoral duty of bishops to encourage and support theologians in their work. The task of theologians in our time is one of extreme difficulty and delicacy. Great and theologically uncharted areas of new knowledge have to be explored, novel problems and difficulties have to be faced; and some of these new tasks are such that only partial guidance can be derived from earlier theologians in tackling them. It would be a poor service to the Church and to the faith and to the faithful if one were to give the impression that one believed there were no problems in theology or scripture, or that they were not serious and worrying, or that it was disloyal or wrong to raise them. The relation of bishops with theologians must, in all fairness, honesty and truth, and above all in Christian charity, contain a strong component of tolerance and patience and sympathy and support.

Sympathy and support for theologians should be forthcoming, not only from bishops but also from the pastoral clergy. The major and better part of modern theology is positive, inspiring, indeed, in the best sense of that word, traditional. It would be both folly and tragedy to reject what the new theology offers us. There are new approaches, new emphases in all the sacred sciences, which, properly understood and assimilated, are an immense enrichment of the faith and a force for renewal of preaching, catechetics and all forms of pastoral care. There are new insights and even new discoveries in scripture study, which, responsibly presented and properly understood, can give a new certitude to our faith and a new depth to our prayer. This new knowledge, coming from the same Word who, from the beginning, enlightens every man, can give joy and peace in believing. We need our theologians and scripture scholars to enable us to assimilate this new knowledge with gratitude to the Holy Spirit. To refuse this knowledge, or to reject the theologians who can mediate it to us, would be to 'resist the Spirit'. Bishops and priests further need the help of theologians in many new pastoral tasks of today's Church. We need them, for example, in the great task which lies before us of continuing theological education. We need them in the related and urgent new task of the adult religious education of the laity.

Some few theologians have, unfortunately, presented this new knowledge in an irresponsible way, as if their function were to shock rather than to edify – though this, on the whole, is more true of the popularisers than of theologians proper. Perhaps also theologians could have done more to help both clergy and faithful to relate the new to the old and to show how both come from the same treasure of God's revelation once given to his Church.

It is, however, possible that some part of the confusion and unease in the Church today comes from the fact that these new questions could not be so openly discussed by Catholic theologians and scholars until the very recent past, so that we have now to concentrate into a few years the debates of several generations. However, the crisis is by no means confined to the Catholic Church and there is little sign that other Churches are affected by it less or are coping with it better.

It must also be allowed for that, in this decade, as distinct from any previous decade, theological discussions simply cannot be confined to specialist circles or reserved to specialist journals. Every such discussion is zealously monitored by journalists, some of whom seem to have radar equipment programmed to pick up signals of sensation, dissent and controversy. Theological thinking is, therefore, frequently presented to the mass audience in a form completely devoid of religious sensitivity or theological nuance, often indeed in a form in which the author can no longer recognise himself.

For all these reasons it is at this time the duty of us all, and of the hierarchy and the theologians specifically, to create an atmosphere of reciprocal confidence in which the assured results of new theological and scriptural scholarship can be assimilated by the whole Church and turned, as it can be and must be, into new fruits of prayer and service and sanctity.

The contribution of theologians to this task is indispensable and the service they can render to the Church is immense. Father Roderick MacKenzie remarks:

In the present situation, the nature of things being what it is, the scholar will rarely find at the end of his journey either popularity or high ecclesiastical office. In the long run he renders to the Church an indispensable service by the exercise of a charism which no-one possesses but himself. This is how the Spirit calls him to cooperate in building up the Church in charity.[17]

As well as deserving encouragement and support from bishops, theologians nowadays will often also need to be defended by them from unjust attack. There are undoubtedly elements of 'intégrisme' or extreme conservatism, to be found in many countries at present, and Ireland is not immune from their attentions. These circles are not numerous, but they are indefatigable and display a zeal which one would dearly wish to see used for more constructive purposes. Unfortunately the extremism of many of these groups cuts them off from the main stream of life in the post-conciliar Church. Their good faith need not be doubted; and undeniably their reactions often spring from genuine pain and justified outrage at the irresponsible utterances which have come from some theologians or publicists. In all honesty, it must be admitted that things have been done and said in the Church in recent years which must shock and sadden everyone who loves the Church and the faith. If we have not been saddened and shocked, this could be because we have not loved the Church and the faith enough.

But when all this has been said, nothing justifies the tone and the tactics of the 'intégristes'. Their movement is by no means to be regarded as a salutary check on the excesses of radicalism, or as providing a needed counter-weight to balance the radical theological wing. It is, on the contrary, a menace of at least equal gravity. It is every whit as critical and corrosive of lawful Church authority, every bit as intolerant and divisive as is radicalism. It creates problems for the Church's magisterium little different from those created by 'radicalism'. It damages both unity in faith and communion in charity in the Church. It is just as lacking in the charity without which no-one can

[17] Art. cit. in *Theology of Renewal*, vol. II, p. 132. The present writer may be permitted to query whether 'popularity' and 'high ecclesiastical office' should thus be bracketed together. Theologians should perhaps rather be congratulated if they succeed in escaping the second!

witness to Christ's truth or build up his Church. Theologians, scripture scholars and catechists can rightly look to bishops for support against unjust criticisms from such sources. Priests and people should not be misled into unnecessary panic or into unjust judgments about theologians because of accusations emanating from such sources. These accusations are frequently based upon quotations taken out of context. Frequently also the accusations simply reflect unawareness of the real problems which exist and which theologians cannot ignore.

This is not to deny that there are abuses by theologians of their new-found freedom. It is the obligation of bishops – and Pope Paul and the Synod of Bishops have reminded us frequently of it – to reprove error and to teach sound doctrine. But it can scarcely be doubted that we bishops will do this more convincingly if we have first shown awareness of the grave and difficult problems which theologians have to face, if we have manifested sympathy and support for theologians in their task, and have thereby gained the confidence of theologians.

THE IRISH THEOLOGICAL COMMISSION

The Irish bishops showed their confidence in theologians and their desire for collaboration with them when in 1972 they set up the Theological Commission. This Commission provides the basic structures necessary for mutually fruitful and beneficial collaboration between theologians and the hierarchy. Already the Theological Commission has rendered invaluable service in the drafting of preliminary texts to serve as the basis for eventual Pastoral Letters; in theological evaluation of important statements of a doctrinal character, such as the Agreed Statements on the Eucharist and on the Ministry emanating from the International Anglican-Roman Catholic Commission, and in the preparation of submissions of a theological character for the Synod of Bishops. This work, valuable in itself and valuable also for the fostering of a new climate of cooperation and coresponsibility, will continue and will be even more vigorously promoted in future. The same will for collaboration is shown in the recent setting up of a newly re-constituted Advisory Committee on Ecumenism.

In this and other ways the Irish bishops have been saying and will go on saying to theologians what Pope Paul said to them in 1966, in a style probably without precedent in the whole history of the Papacy:

> Do not refuse to help us in our task of maintaining and defending Catholic truth and witnessing publicly to it. Give to Us and our brothers in the episcopate your fraternal help in this task. We have great confidence in your work, because we are convinced that your collaboration will make less heavy and more fruitful the commission given by our Lord to Us and to the whole Episcopal College, the commission to guard faithfully the deposit of Catholic doctrine, to preach the faith and to spread ever more vigorously the name of Christ.[18]

THEOLOGIANS IN RELATION TO ONE ANOTHER

There are so many tasks facing theologians today that it seems invidious to point to some duties as specially important. But there is justification for urging upon them one rather neglected task of charitably and justly but openly and firmly criticising one another when truth requires it. Some leading theologians of our time have both advocated and practised this task of 'fraternal correction' between theologians. Father Congar has more than once recently reiterated his conviction that, in the present situation of enforced comparative abeyance of the traditional methods for safeguarding orthodoxy in the Church, it is a duty of theologians to criticise a fellow-theologian when they feel he is mistaken or is even endangering the faith or the unity of the Church. In a period when the magisterium can scarcely attempt any longer to prevent the publication and diffusion of theological error and when, in any case, interventions of authority can scarcely any longer be effective or final, new ways must be found

[18] *Documentation Catholique,* col. 1742.

of 'guarding the deposit'. One of these must be the exposing of theological error by theologians themselves. Pope Paul has called for the exercise of 'fraternal correction' in the course of his appeal for reconciliation within the Church.[19]

At present, theologians rarely criticise one another in public. Books which are plainly in error or subversive of the faith are rarely exposed as such in theological articles or reviews. They are sometimes given uncritical or even flattering reviews in religious periodicals. Part of the reason may be that theologians tend to see themselves as threatened by authority and as needing to show solidarity with one another in preparedness to resist moves of authority against their freedom. This is surely an attitude unworthy of those who are entrusted with handling the saving word of God. One would hope that, if more confident and trusting relationships are mutually fostered, such an attitude would become more uncommon. If bishops can involve theologians more in sharing their responsibility for the teaching of sound doctrine, one would hope that theologians will themselves come to feel that they are responsible in their sphere, just as much as bishops are in theirs, for the faithful transmission of 'the faith once delivered to the saints'.

Another necessity for theologians nowadays is to broaden the range of their dialogue, not only with one another and with scholars in other disciplines, and not only with theologians of other communions – and in these areas dialogue is nowadays happily commonplace – but with non-theologians, with the pastoral clergy, with religious, with contemplatives and with men and women of simple faith and prayer and Christian witness. Without such contacts theology can easily become theologians' theology, couched in rather esoteric jargon. It can become too much a verbal, cerebral exercise, out of touch with reality and with the actual life and prayer of the Church and the people of God. This is greatly to the damage of theology itself as well as of its service to the Church.

[19] *Reconciliation within the Church*, sect. 6, p. 27.

Some secularising theologians were still solemnly asking, 'Can prayer be theologically justified?', at the very time when it was reckoned that there were some ten thousand young French people in India, looking for gurus to teach them to pray, because they could not find theologians or priests at home to teach them; at a time when tens of thousands of young people from all continents were flocking to Taizé, not to discuss the theology of prayer, but to pray; and when all over the world prayer groups were spontaneously forming in which people, oblivious to all the arguments demonstrating that, being 'modern secular men come of age', they need not and could not pray, at least in any sense of prayer as hitherto understood – were simply praying. To all of us who were or are professional teachers of philosophical theology or of theology it must stand as a rebuke that the massive return to prayer all over the Church happened without us; and for long was unnoticed by many of us.

In the new situation in the Church it is necessary for theologians to preserve a great humility. Nobody nowadays has any right to be so sure that he is right and all others wrong as some theologians, and some critics of theologians, seem now to be. Roderick MacKenzie names humility with integrity as the chief components of the charism which the theological scholar has to put at the service of the Church. He asks his fellow-scholars, in the name of both virtues, to be ready to say, if the occasion demands it, 'I was wrong'.[20] Hans Kueng in 1965 made a similar appeal. He wrote:

> The theologian who is thinking and working critically will always and everywhere have plenty of grounds for humility.[21]

But it is St Paul who has the message most relevant to the contemporary situation of the theologian. It will be found in Chapter XII of his first letter to the Corinthians, in the context of the variety of charisms in the one body of Christ which is the Church.

---

[20] *Theology of Renewal*, vol. I, p. 132.
[21] *The Theologian and the Church*, p. 31.

Despite the cynicism of Kierkegaard in respect of 'professors of theology', we can surely claim that theologians are included in St Paul's list of charisms. They are surely envisaged at least implicitly among those who have 'the gift of preaching with wisdom given [them] by the Spirit', 'the gift of preaching instruction given [them] by the same Spirit', and 'the gift of faith given by the same Spirit' (1 *Corinthians* 12:8-10). Theologians surely have also their place among the 'prophets' and 'teachers' in his second list (1 *Corinthians* 12:28-29).

What St Paul stresses is that all these gifts are given for the service of the Church and are to be valued only insofar as they promote the unity of the Church in love. The different categories and charisms cannot exist except in dependence on one another and cannot serve the body of the Church without the support of one another. The logic of St Paul certainly suggests that teachers cannot serve the Church without apostles, nor apostles without teachers; neither can theologians without bishops, nor bishops without theologians. There should be 'no disagreements inside the body, but each part [should] be equally concerned for all the others' (1 *Corinthians* 12:25). Neither group should hurt the other or derive any sort of satisfaction from the other's loss or pain. 'If one part is hurt, all parts are hurt with it. If one part is given special honour, all parts enjoy it' (1 *Corinthians* 12:28). It is true that bishops might sometimes well wonder whether their critics suppose they have no feelings at all and are immune from personal hurt. But we bishops in turn must be equally concerned about the capacity of theologians to feel hurt. If, before writing or speaking, we were all to remember the words of St Paul, 'If one part is hurt, all parts are hurt with it', the tone of our exchanges and our conversations might be very different. Father Congar writes very impressively of attempting 'to be open to new discoveries and new questions and also to approach all men with an *a priori* of love and of trust'.[22]

It is above all in the liturgy that we will find the grace and the

[22] *Une passion, L'unité*, p. iii.

motivation and the model for that working together in love which all of us in the modern Church, and specifically theologians and bishops, must pursue. It is Father Congar again who says:

> Above all else I want to keep myself faithfully in the tradition of the apostles and the saints. I believe strongly . . . in the strengthening and the regulating of the faith and of life and conduct by the practice of the liturgy. The liturgy has opened for me the best doors for the perception of the mysteries and for access to the peace which is the free gift of the Spirit of God.[23]

Father Chantraine has pointed out that in the Eucharist we have a twofold self-giving of Jesus: he gives himself first in his Gospel; then he gives himself in his body and blood. Over both of these self-givings it is the successors of his Twelve Apostles who preside. Both doctrine and Eucharist are part of the charge which Christ entrusted to the apostles. By Christ's doctrine taught and Christ's Eucharist celebrated in union with the successors of the apostles, the Church keeps her trust with Christ.[24] Nobody insisted on this twofold truth more than St Ignatius of Antioch. He says:

> Take a fresh grip on your faith (the very flesh of the Lord) and your love (the life-blood of Jesus Christ) . . .
> I am clinging for refuge to the gospel message, as to the Christ, and to the Apostles as the collective mystery of the Church.

We are saved by Hope

The above two quotations from St Ignatius of Antioch are found in the new breviary. This latter is in itself a good example of both the difficulties and the values of true renewal. The renewal of the 'Liturgy of the Hours' took nearly ten years of patient work. Meanwhile some grew impatient and some, here and there, gave up praying the breviary. If only we could learn how

---

[23] Loc. cit.
[24] G. Chantraine: *Vraie et fausse liberté due theologien*, Desclée de Brouwer, 1969, pp. 143.

to wait! The waiting in this case has been abundantly repaid. The new breviary has the potential to lead towards holiness a whole generation of priests, religious, and laity. We have only to recall how a whole generation all over the Church was helped to holiness by the writings of Abbot Marmion – all of whose doctrine derived from prayerful reflection upon the contents of his breviary and upon his Mass.

This is only one example of the need for patience and the reward of patience. Ours is a privileged generation. It is tonic to hear Father Congar acclaim the Vatican Council as the fulfilment of all the hopes of a lifetime. If we re-read Hans Kueng's pre-conciliar writings, we will have to grant that practically all that he demanded of the Council has been fulfilled by Vatican II and by the unswervingly faithful implementation of it by Pope Paul VI. Before we begin to think of Vatican III, let us first exploit the treasures and the opportunities of Vatican II. The Spirit is at work in the Church today and in our world today. If we could only read the signs of our times we would say of so much that is happening today what St Peter said to the crowd on the first Pentecost: '[Jesus] has received from the Father the Holy Spirit, who was promised, and what you see and hear is the outpouring of that Spirit' (*Acts* 2:33). If we can only learn to wait, we will see marvellous things from the Spirit's sowing.

Father Congar speaks of 'active patience'. He describes it as:

something quite different from a mere passive waiting, a letting time go by vacantly. It is rather a quality of spirit or of soul, which is rooted in the deep and lived conviction, first that God is in charge and that he is carrying out through us his design of grace; secondly, that, for all great works, a time for maturing is necessary . . . it is the patient sower, who entrusts his grain to the earth and the sun, who is the man of hope. 'If a man knows how to wait, everything will be revealed to him in the end, provided that he has the courage not to deny in the darkness what he has seen in the light' (Coventry Patmore).[25]

It is on the solid rock-substratum of faith that our sure hope is founded; and neither problems nor pluralisms in theology can disturb or move this rock of faith. As Newman put it, 'ten thousand difficulties do not make one doubt'. Ten thousand articles by theologians do not carry the weight of one single article of the Creed – because the latter rests on God's word, not on theologians' learning or reputation. It is well for us all to remember that, if speculation by theologians is 'of human origin, it will break up of its own accord'; but what is of faith 'comes from God' and human speculation or dissent or doubt 'will be unable to destroy [it]', for these would be 'fighting against God' (*Acts* 5:38-39). We have incomparably more reason for this serene and patient certainty that Gamaliel had, for 'we have seen Christ's glory, the glory that is his as the only Son of the Father, full of grace and truth' (*John* 1:14).

More and more we must remember nowadays that hope, like love, is an essential part of Christian orthodoxy. If deploring the state of the Church were to weaken hope, it would also be undermining faith. Also, if criticism of theologians, whether by bishops or by anyone else, were so conducted as to offend charity, it would be contradicting true faith as well: because it is ultimately in 'God's love towards ourselves . . . that we have put our faith'. Pope Paul in his December 1974 appeal for Reconciliation in the Church during the Holy Year, to which reference was made above, ends with these words:

> [The Church] wishes to change also the sorrow which has been visited upon her into a love that can understand everything and in Christ pardon everything.

St Paul says:

> If I have the gift of prophecy, understanding all the mysteries there are, and knowing everything . . . but without love, then I am nothing at all.

[25] *Une Passion, L'unité*, p. 82-83.

He ends his whole passage about hierarchy and charisms in the Church by the words:

There are three things that last: faith, hope and love; and the greatest of these is love (1 *Corinthians* 13:2-13).